Passive Income Blueprint:

Your Roadmap To Financial Freedom

By: Kelvin Wang DX

Legal & Disclaimer

The information contained in this book and its contents is not designed to replace or take the place of any form of medical or professional advice; and is not meant to replace the need for independent medical, financial, legal or other professional advice or services, as may be required. The content and information in this book have been provided for educational and entertainment purposes only.

The content and information contained in this book have been compiled from sources deemed reliable, and it is accurate to the best of the Author's knowledge, information, and belief. However, the Author cannot guarantee its accuracy and validity and cannot be held liable for any errors and/or omissions. Further, changes are periodically made to this book as and when needed. Where appropriate and/or necessary, you must consult a professional (including but not limited to your doctor, attorney, financial advisor or such other professional advisor) before using any of the suggested remedies, techniques, or information in this book.

Upon using the contents and information contained in this book, you agree to hold harmless the Author from and against any damages, costs, and expenses, including any legal fees potentially resulting from the application of any of the information provided by this book. This disclaimer applies to any loss, damages or injury caused by the use and application, whether directly or indirectly, of any advice or information presented, whether for breach of contract, tort, negligence, personal injury, criminal intent, or under any other cause of action.

You agree to accept all risks of using the information presented inside this book.

You agree that by continuing to read this book, where appropriate and/or necessary, you shall consult a professional (including but not limited to your doctor, attorney, or financial advisor or such other advisor as needed) before using any of the suggested remedies, techniques, or information in this book.

Table of Contents

Contents

Introduction

The idea of earning passive income has been around for ages. You surely have folks or relatives earning a decent amount of money from their real estate properties. That's exactly the time-tested way of earning a passive income. But as times are changing, people discover that earning a steady passive income is not limited to rental properties or business activities that do not require material participation, as per the Internal Revenue Service's definition.

With a lot of money-making opportunities out there, it's impossible not to find an opportunity that will allow you to earn passive income nowadays. The best way to learn how to launch and grow a passive income stream is to find out how the successful ones do it. In this book, we compiled the secrets of the top passive income earners. How did they begin it? What are their strategies to keep the business going?

You surely have heard some of the new passive income streams, like investing in dividend stocks and peer to peer lending. My goal is to supplement what you already know by providing you the best practices to these fields. That way, you can start your journey of having a reliable, long-term source of passive income. Who does not want financial freedom and live the life they always wanted? I am here to help you get started your journey to financial freedom, with the help of passive income streams.

Chapter 1: What is Passive Income?

Passive Income is defined as the income obtained with little time and effort needed to maintain it. It is a regular income coming from another source other than a contractor or an employer. According to the American Internal Revenue Service, it is one of the three broad types of income. The other two are active income and portfolio income. Active income is acquired through services performed like compensation or salary. Portfolio income is obtained through dividends, investments, royalties, capital gains, and interest. Passive income is sometimes drawing similarities to portfolio income because it can be in the form of an interest from a bank account; royalties from music, computer software, or books; stock dividends; Internet ads on websites; and pensions.

The IRS limits passive income to rental properties and trade or business that does not require people to materially participate. Once you engage in a trade or business activity for more than 500 hours, it is "material participation." The IRS will not consider you as a passive income earner if you are involved in a business for more than an hour the entire taxable year.

There are financial and government institutions that do not agree with IRS' definition of passive income. Like I mentioned earlier, there are so many passive income sources out there waiting for you to explore and the first on the list is in the succeeding chapter. I like how these ideas make it easy to start a business with little to no capital at all.

Is passive income taxable? The good news is that the tax rates of passive income are lower than that of active income. As per the federal government's ruling, an active income or those derived from wages and salaries fall at 35 percent while passive income is at 15 percent. While it makes sense that earning passive income requires little effort to keep it going, you will actually need to exert time, hard work, and effort if you want to build real wealth out of it. Truth is, creating passive income is not a passive activity. Do note that some activities are just more passive than others. Contrary to popular belief, earning a passive income is not a get rich quick scheme or as laidback as sitting in a coffee shop while you enjoy sipping your favorite Frappuccino. It requires lots of work, time, and even resources for it to succeed.

Does it mean that you have to go to a complicated process before you can earn a steady passive income? It can be laborious in the beginning, yes, especially when you are just getting started. But once you get the hang of it, you will discover that there are ways to make it a little less complicated. How? Automate and outsource. These are two of the best ways to keep your business running. As the name suggests, outsourcing refers to a good or service obtained from an outside supplier. You might have come across websites that allow you to outsource workers. Automating work, on the other hand, requires applications and services to get started.

Chapter 2: Are passive income really achievable?

The answer is yes! Because it exists for quite some time now, the idea of earning passive income is not questionable. Many people around the globe are enjoying their steady flow of passive income. I, myself, have friends who earn cash while they sleep. The real question here is how you can make it happen in your own life. In this chapter, I will share with you how successful passive income earners get to the top of their game. These are four strategies real passive income earners do.

Visualizing success

Successful passive income earners imagine success and work for it. Pat Flynn, a passive income whiz who founded SmartPassiveIncome.com believes success is not accidental. He believes people should have at least one adage that would reflect people and his is "the harder you work, the luckier you become." Think of the law of attraction. When you think of success as something not bound to happen, you will eventually shudder at working a little harder. But if you believe that success is for you, the universe will help you get through it. Luck, in the end, is not by chance but the choices we make.

Understanding your niche

These people don't serve just anybody or everybody. Anyone running a successful business knows the importance of understanding a good niche. It's all about being clear about what you want to offer. What are these products and services? Who is your target market? For example, you want to launch a new website about fashion and makeup. Your target market would be young girls who have the purchasing power. So basically, you focus on fashion and makeup. After understanding a good niche, it's time to identify the needs of your customers.

Evaluating people's needs and wants

Successful passive income earners focus on their customer's needs. Later in this book, I will give you more insights about creating digital products and how you can earn passive income from them. Let's say you are planning to write an eBook. Perhaps you already have your business plan and you have an idea what you would include on your eBook chapters. But have you asked your ideal readers what they actually want or need? It takes some courage to ask and if you're not yet ready for something like this, it is fine to join Facebook groups and see what your ideal clients are talking about. I join several Facebook groups on my niche. I participate in the discussions.

Creating a logical plan

Let's say you are planning to open an online shop and sell items from home. You cannot decide whether you will create your own product or source from a manufacturer. Creating your own product works when you already master it and it will not be time-consuming. Examples are digital products like eBooks.

You learned that sourcing product is more convenient and time-saving. So you contacted manufacturers. They helped you have the products you need for your online shop. Later on, you learned that the manufacturer is willing to send those orders directly to your buyers. All you needed to do is get their information. That refers to drop shipping and that will be tackled in one chapter of this book.

I mentioned drop shipping because I wanted to emphasize how hard it is to make choices in launching a new venture. This is where planning comes into the picture. I recommend that you have a business plan before you begin. I heard so many stories of people failing with their startups not because the business was not profitable enough but because they did not have the right strategy. They suffer from information overload. A business plan can help you organize your thoughts and be clear about your goals.

A business plan that works has a heart-centered approach. What does it mean? Michael E. Gerber, a New York Times best-selling author and entrepreneur, described it as an approach that starts with experiencing the feelings you have. This is far cry from the traditional business plan that is normally head-centric, meaning it begins with logics, thoughts, and reasons.

Chapter 3: Dividend's stock investment

The steady payments are the number one reason why many people put money into dividend-paying stocks. What are dividend stocks, if you may ask? The dividend is the payment made by a corporation to its shareholders. However, companies do not always distribute payouts in cash. There are times when they distribute additional stocks to their shareholders and this is what we meant by stock dividends. The returns in dividend investing are usually small but you can increase the value by selling stocks.

Want to invest in dividend stocks? As a beginner, invest in low volatility stocks first. Just because a stock is high-yielding means it will produce a high total return. Those who wish to create a stable growing dividend income should reconsider about taking big risks at the very start. There are reasons why there are high dividend stocks and one of this is an underlying business problem.

If that is the case then how are you going to choose the best dividend stocks? Many investors would agree that the secret lies in the long-term success of a company. Here are questions you might want to research when choosing a dividend investing strategy:

- What is the financial health of the company?
- Does the company have the ability to increase its payout over time?
- How does the management treat their investors?
- Does the company have an excellent credit rating?

Dividend investing is ideal for people with long-term prospects. How long should it be? Warren Buffett, one of the most successful investors in the world, believes the best holding period for stocks is "forever."

I mentioned management in the questions above. I want to emphasize the importance of researching their historical treatment of dividends. Did the company face a difficult financial time? How did the management handle it? You will realize that there are more questions you will ask in the long run because the management has a huge impact on the financial health of a company. I agree with Buffett's belief that a stock should be kept as long as possible.

Chapter 4: Rental properties

Owning a rental property can be both a blessing and a curse. It's no secret that there are tenants from hell or those who demand a lot and pay late. But let's focus on the powerful, beautiful side of having a real estate property of your own. Rental properties are one of the earliest known sources of passive income. Nowadays, people would rather rent spaces than deal with the increasing rate of property tax and if you already have a property, you can use it as an asset. As an owner of a rental property, take into considerations these important factors to guarantee passive income in the long run.

Rental property maintenance

Basically, it's unfair to set a high rental rate when the property is in bad shape. Maintenance works are one of the dreaded tasks of homeowners. But if you're planning to rent it out, this is really something you need to do unless you decided to rent it out at a cheap price. Before charging more for rent, make sure that the house is well-maintained. Do some repaint, refinish the inside, or do some landscaping to the yard.

New Ways to Create listings

Airbnb is a marketplace where travelers can list, discover, and book unique accommodations around the world. You can be a host and rent out your extra space by signing up to marketplaces like Airbnb. A list serves as a profile page of your place. Airbnb is a good place to start hosting your property.

Finding the right neighborhood

If you are still planning to buy a property for rental purposes, spend a lot of time finding the right one. Joseph Hogue, an investment analyst, believes it is a huge mistake to buy and rent out a property in a lower-income neighborhood. Some people think they will eventually get a huge discount when they buy a property that costs half less than better areas. Unpaid rent and repairs alone can be the two factors why it's not ideal to buy a property in the low-income neighborhood and have it rented out.

Putting your rentals in Limited Liability Companies (LLC)

LLCs protect investors from liability on rental properties. The risk is always part of owning a rental property and whether you like it or not, that property is vulnerable to potential lawsuits. Your assets will eventually be affected when the property is under your name. When thinking of putting your property in LLC, research its pros and cons first. Ask a legal expert and determine whether an LLC is for you.

Owning a rental property can be a rewarding experience. It will surely give you steady passive income just as long as you have the right strategy.

Chapter 5: Peer to Peer Lending Platform

Peer to Peer lending or crowdlending is the practice of lending money to individuals or businesses through online services that match lenders directly with borrowers. Here's an example of how it works: You wanted to open a small gift shop and you need around $30,000 for the startup. Because you have insufficient funds to cover all the startup expenses, you went to a bank to apply for a loan. You presented your business model. However, the bank was not impressed with your idea and rejected your proposal.

While looking for an alternative, you stumbled upon a crowdlending website. The website allowed you to borrow the capital you need. Investor A lends you $25, Investor Blends $100, and so on until you reached $30,000. The crowdlending website split the investment across a range of borrowers to reduce the risk. This is called Notes.

These lenders earn cash thru interest. If you are interested in starting a P2P business, automated investing sites are the best way to go. P2P is a rising business these days because P2P online platforms make it more convenient to borrow money. Banks are stricter when it comes to checking credentials. Applying for a bank loan can take up to three months while borrowing thru P2P can take approximately 12 days.

Online credit marketplace like Prosper.com and Lending Club evaluates the client information for you. These platforms will match you directly on borrowers based on certain criteria. All you have to do is select loans in which to invest.

How much can you earn through P2P lending? Returns vary depending on the platform. These automated investing sites will calculate how much you could earn on a Note. The more notes that you invest in, the higher the returns. There are various factors that influence returns.

What is the risk in P2P? Any loan has risks involved. There is no security in P2P. You will lose money when the borrowers failed to pay. The good thing about joining an online credit marketplace is that they could help you collect payments in case the borrower missed a payment. How will you lower the potential for losses? Spread out your investment through a variety of borrowers.

While there are risks involved, P2P lending can be a win-win situation for both lenders and borrowers when done right. Borrowers can apply without a hassle. Those who borrowed to launch their business can repay the loan while growing their ventures. Lenders can choose who to lend to while enjoying a steady stream of passive income.

Chapter 6: EBook Publishing Business

The publishing world is changing really fast. Gone were the days when people have to go through a scrutiny of a publishing company before seeing their book printed. Nowadays, you can sell your book without too much hassle and earn royalties from it. More and more people are taking advantage of self-publishing. Living in a fast-paced world can be a good thing, too. Almost all people choose to read straight from their smartphones and tablets and this can be a money-making opportunity. Even those newspaper and magazine publishers are relying on digital subscriptions from their readers.

Start as an infopreneur. What is an infopreneur? Tim Ferriss' "The Four Hour Work Week" is one of the best-selling books about passive income. If you already read the book, you surely know that Ferriss wants you to kill the nine to five and escape the office. But it was also noticeable that in the book, Ferriss stressed two things: the importance of information products and selecting a niche you know. By information products, Ferriss means eBooks, blogs, and podcasts or anything that enlightens people.

You can start your journey as an "infopreneur" by self-publishing or create a digital product like an eBook. How much can you earn by writing e-Books? This is perhaps the biggest question you have in mind right now. Your possible earnings vary from platform to platform. You can sell the book from $.99 up to $19. You can also sell it on your own website. Apparently, the price should depend on the quality and quantity of a book. Before self-publishing, your book, take note of these five important considerations.

Conduct a market research.

Sadly, this is one of the important factors that some authors ignore. If you want to write an eBook that sells, it matters to conduct your research. It is not hard as it looks like. Start your own group of friends. Interview these people. Are they concerned most about their dating life? Write about tips on maintaining relationships. Are they asking you advice about handling finances? Write about wealth. Other than wealth and relationship topics, health and personal passions are the other niches that sell.

Provide value.

You might be tempted to start with a self-help book because self-improvement is such a big business. Do note that not all self-help books work. A self-help book should be backed by science for it to be effective. Providing value can also be done by focusing on "how to." The number of topics is endless and you are more on the safe side. How-to topics work because it creates curiosity.

Familiarize yourself with proper formatting.

Digital platforms like Amazon's Kindle and Barnes and Noble's Nook have strict standards when it comes to formatting eBooks. Save it to PDF before sending it to the publishers who could help you convert it into epub format. Aside from following the correct format, it's also a must to have an attractive cover. It's important that you have the relevant images to attract readers. You may want to hire a freelancer who could help you design your eBook cover. Believe me, there are simplistic eBooks that made it simply because of the eBook design. It's normal for people to judge based on appearance. So exert a bit more on the cover or get help from experts.

Think outside the box

If you want to create fiction books such as science fiction, fantasy, and romance, be extra-creative. Read books and watch movies in your favorite genre. Go out, walk, and talk to people. I do these when I am out of inspiration to write. There are so many things you can do to unleash creativity. Sometimes, the creative juice is flowing at the least expected time so I suggest that you keep a notepad and a pen in handy just in case. I have to say that fiction books are more complicated to write unless of course, you really have the talent in writing.

Chapter 7: YouTube channel

For you to earn money from your videos, you will need to join the YouTube Partner Program. From there, set up your AdSense account. It's actually easier to apply for an AdSense account for YouTube than for a blog or website. Just make sure that your account is enabled for monetization. Once you become a "host account" or your account has been approved for AdSense and you get hits, expect to receive your payment once it exceeded $100. You can also choose which videos you want to monetize.

YouTube determines your earnings depending on the type of ads and their pricing. Take note that there are types of videos that are not eligible. AdSense is strict when it comes to commercial rights, so try to make everything as original as possible. If, in case, you really need to use a certain music as background, provide a proper attribution. Also take note that monetization is currently not available to all countries. You may want to check first if your country is allowed to have it. Check their copyright and community guidelines.

Now there are only two things you need to ask yourself before monetizing your YouTube channel. First, do you have an audience? Second, can you create engaging videos on a regular basis? If the answer to these questions is yes, it's time for you to get started but let's discuss these two factors first.

Audience before the income. This is a golden rule if you want to start earning a passive income from your YouTube channel. Growing your audience requires learning about Search Engine Optimization or SEO. For a video to be discovered, it should have searchable titles. Let's say you have a baking channel. If I were the one searching for a certain no-bake recipe, I would rather click a headline that says "Easy 3-Ingredient No-Bake Dessert" than the one that says "No-bake peanut butter dessert." The secret in creating a catchy title is to be creative while keeping the necessary keywords on your title.

The last and perhaps, the more important thing to consider, is your capability to produce YouTube videos on a regular basis. Once you have an audience or subscribers, these people will surely wait for your next video. Invest in a good camera and learn about video editing software. It matters to have good audio as well, so you might want to invest in a decent mic.

Chapter 8: Online Coaching Business

Interactions and connections are the two most important factors to keep in mind when starting an online coaching business. Basically, you don't want people to think that you're there just because you want their money. People will not trust you unless they know you and they like you.

Having a real-life accomplishment on a certain niche is one big advantage in starting an online coaching business. For example, you've been training people to be fit for years now. Use your previous experience to be an online fitness coach. Establish yourself as an expert. How will you do this? Start by focusing on a niche service. When you coach a niche you are passionate about, it's given that you will attract the right clients.

Judy Jablon, an early childhood consultant says there are three steps in powerful interaction. The first is being present which means you say and do things with effectiveness and maximum clarity. The second one is a connection. You should have a deeper relationship with the person you're coaching. The third and most important step is extend learning. Have you thought the person the best practices to attach to those learnings?

Now your goal is to let people know about you. How to get other people know you before presenting your services? Show your face or do a Facebook Live coaching. Have a well-written "About Me" page. Share your stories. Making people like you is another story. I know one strategy that works. Be relatable. Notice how we like people who have something in common with us? Like, someone who has the same name as us. People tend to be more comfortable with what they know because an "unfamiliar territory" is basically hard to trust. Being liked is one way to influence people. Once you get people like you, building trust is not that hard to achieve at all.

As a coach, your audience expects a lot from you like you are the type of person who makes the best decisions in life. If you, yourself is facing some life issues and you don't have any help, you won't likely meet that expectation. Remember, how you are and what you say will affect how others think about you. You can grow your coaching business through social media and blogging. Create helpful and inspiring content on a regular basis.

Chapter 9: Affiliate Marketing

Affiliate marketing is endorsing other people's products and services and getting a compensation after successfully referring others. Aside from receiving a percentage of the sale, it's also possible to get a fixed amount per every lead. A lead does not necessarily purchase but uses your affiliate link to sign up. Most affiliate programs will require you to have a blog or a website. There are also some that only require a social page. Below are 10 of the best affiliate programs that you may use whether you are a newbie or an experienced blogger.

1. Amazon- as their associate, Amazon will give you the access to their programs and earn up to 6% on local referrals. They also offer up to 75% discounts on products and local services.
2. SiteGround- it is by far one of the best hosting companies these days. For every referral, they will pay you $65.
3. Shareasale- what I like most about this affiliate network is that they will pay you for every lead and every sale. They offer $1 per lead and a generous $100 per sale. I recommend this to publishers looking for a decent pay-per-lead program.
4. eBay- their in-house affiliate program gives as much as 200% referral bonus for new or reactivated buyers. Once accepted, you will have access to eBay's Publisher Portal where you could get banners, text links, and buttons. You can use these on your websites and even social pages.
5. Rakuten Linkshare- dubbed as the global leader in performance marketing, they require you have a loyal following on your website before you can sign up. Work on your blog and strive to get as many hits as possible.
6. Viglink- as a publisher, you will get a snippet code that will automatically turn existing links on your page into revenue generating links. You will earn a commission once a user makes a purchase.
7. Ideal Shape- this weight loss website will pay you $10 for every blog post you write about their products or website.
8. Clickbank- you will be given a unique link that you can use to promote products. They will give you a free book that you can use as a guide.
9. FlexOffers- they have thousands of products- right from clothing and accessories down to online and legal services that you can promote on your website. Once you become a publisher, you can also earn money by referring new publishers to their network.
10. AWeber- it is free to join in this email marketing program. You could earn up to 30% lifetime recurring commission per referral. They pay through Check.

Affiliate marketing is not limited to cash. Some merchants render huge discounts as compensation for every customer you bring in. This is also called a referral program. Take note that referral program and affiliate marketing program also have few differences. In referral program, the goal is to promote something to make people's lives better while in affiliate marketing, your goal is to earn a living for yourself. Some companies provide discounts when you sign up or refer customers. These are some of the merchants that offer rewards other than cash. While these will not give you passive income, you can take advantage of the rewards to save some cash.

1. Dropbox- this file hosting service lets you store all your photos, videos, and files in one place. You can also access them anywhere. When you have a free account, you only have around 2GB of space. You could earn extra space by referring your friends. You could earn 500 MB per referral when you have a free account and 1 GB per referral when you have a pro account.
2. Evernote- this freemium app is designed for note taking and organizing. You will earn 5 points for every friend you refer. You can use the points to get their Premium account.
3. CriCut- there are affiliates that won't require you to promote. Simply sign up to their program and you will already get a discount. CriCut, an electronic cutting machine brand, offers up to 30% discount to their affiliates.
4. Montage- you will get a free photo book once your review is approved. At least that's something you can keep for a lifetime!
5. Freebie Direct- they will help you offer free stuff to entice site visitors and increase your readership. This can work for both new and mid-level website owners.

When promoting your affiliate programs, never sound like you are advertising it. Create an epic post and mention a certain product. There are creative ways to do it. One effective way to do it is to create an honest review of a certain product. You can do it through a video or through your blog. A product tutorial post will be of great help to readers. Or better, do a mini giveaway.

As a publisher, giving away a freebie will also benefit you because you could build trust. You can also grow your followers by offering the freebie in exchange for their follows and likes. You can also include affiliate links on the giveaway page.

Chapter 10: Drop ship

A drop shipping business is a supply chain management method wherein you don't have to keep goods in stock. Instead, you transfer a customer's shipment details and orders to another retailer or a manufacturer. Drop shipping can be a good source of passive income because it's pretty easy to maintain. But like any business model, it has both pros and cons too.

For now, I want you to focus on the good side of drop shipping. What I like most about drop shipping is that you can do it from home. There is no need to bother about keeping an inventory of stocks and since you don't need to set up a physical store, you have the freedom to offer more items to your buyers. Isn't it more convenient when you don't have to take care of everything? Eventually, someone else is responsible for customer care and shipping the items to the buyer.

You may want to start on Fulfillment by Amazon (FBA). When you already have a "Selling on Amazon" account, simply add FBA and start creating your product listings. Once a customer orders a product, Amazon will be the one picking, packing, and shipping the item. That sounds easy but read all their guidelines to make sure you're doing it right.

On eBay, it is called product sourcing. As a seller, you are not obliged to handle an item. All you have to do is collect the money from the buyer and forward it to a product source. Like the FBA, the product source on eBay will be responsible for sending the item straight to the buyer.

As someone who does business, it matters to find the best partners. This is actually the most challenging part of running a drop shipping business. If the manufacturer, unfortunately, ships the wrong items or if there is a long delay, you will eventually piss off your customers.

You can abstain from such blunder by researching carefully your drop shipping partners. A trustworthy drop shipping supplier does not ask for membership fees or pre-order fees. Genuine suppliers are willing to accept orders via email and they consist of expert staff. Sometimes, it's not enough that you search on Google. Be careful because there are a lot of spammy listings out there. The best way to find a drop shipping wholesaler is to contact the manufacturer directly.

There are a few techniques to have a successful drop shipping business. One strategy is to focus on niche merchandise. It's quite hard to serve everybody. Focus on the group of people who will likely buy your products. Because you provide specific services, there will be less competition so you don't have to bother about marketing too much.

Chapter 11: App Development

You don't need to be a rocket scientist to develop an app. With patience, time, and enthusiasm, I believe there is no reason for you not to learn it. You can even do it right from home without any background in programming. Sounds cool. But, how?

Write down whatever idea you have in mind and create a mockup of that idea using a prototyping tool. As a beginner, it's a must to start with a prototype. A prototyping tool is usually offered for free and will let you test your app without writing any code. You can also use this tool to get feedback from potential customers. Testing the water before releasing a full version an app will save you from potential flops. Some of the well-known prototype websites for apps are Marvel App, InVision, and Fluidui.com.

If you're interested in creating iOS apps for iPhone and iPad, you have to learn about Apple's Swift. This programming language begins with a lesson that enables you to build a simple app. You will get an idea how the code and interface look like at the end of the lesson. For you to create an app using Switch, it's required that you use a Mac computer running the latest version of Xcode. Simply create an Apple ID and download the Xcode for free from the App Store.

Aside from reading Apple's documentation on their programming language, I suggest that you take advantage of free courses and step-by-step tutorials offered by developers. People have different learning styles. Some of us learn better by reading while some by watching videos.

What's next after building an app? It's time to submit it to the App Store. It should be easy since it's the developer's task to upload the app on their website. All you need to do is sign up to the app store and pay the membership fee. The fees vary depending on the app store. Apple requires an annual fee of $99 for individuals and $299 for their enterprise program or those who create organization-exclusive applications. Google only requires a one-time fee of $25 using Google Payments Merchant account. Creating Android apps also requires installing an app called Android Studio. As a beginner, I recommend you join Google's free course on Android development.

Chapter 12: Hobbies

Do you love taking pictures? Then take this hobby as a money-making activity! Yes, you can make money out of your passion for photography. One simple way to do this is to create stock photography.

What is stock photography? It's a supply of pictures that is often licensed for commercial design purposes. Stock photos are usually accessed via online databases and can be bought at a low cost. These databases are like the "supermarket" of photos. With thousands of images at these photo libraries, how will you make your pictures stand out?

Before selling your photos to those websites, make sure that you checked their guidelines first. This is especially important if you are new to this field. It will give you an idea what kind of photos to submit and the subjects these sites are actually looking for.

Speaking of subjects, one study noted that people are attracted to photos showing other people than those that only show abstract or nature. Do note, however, that showing emotion is one of the reasons why these kinds of photo sell. Think of dramatic effects or dynamics. This can be done by mastering the rule of thirds.

In photography terms, this is simplified as the "focal point of a person." The rule of thirds technique is done by putting the main subject either on the left or the right but never in the direct middle of a photo. The alignment produces a sense of direction. This is ideal if you want to create more emotion and dynamics on your photos.

Meanwhile, what if you want to focus on a certain niche? There is nothing bad about it as long as that niche aligns with your passion. For example, you want to pay particular attention to wedding photography. Make sure that you have all the right equipment, like a high-quality DSLR camera, lenses, lens filters, diffuser and reflector kit. Take note that tools differ depending on your niche. The tool needed for food photography can be different from that of wedding photography. It's also a must that you are familiar with photo editing software.

If you are planning to sell your photos, you can start with the help of stock photography agencies. Examples are Evanto Market, Shutterstock, and Fotolia. These agencies buy stock photos. You can earn passive income from the royalties you will get per image. Some agencies even offer referral programs that you could also take advantage of.

Conclusion

If you have decided what type of passive income stream you would like to set up, I would like to congratulate you for it. Stick to those ideas. Who knows, that could be a million dollar idea. That said, all you need to do is an act. Do some action plan and if it fails, don't give up. There are other sources of passive income waiting for you to try. If you still haven't, I hope you could use this book as a reference once day.

I love hearing stories of people earning some pretty good cash while they sleep. They have the freedom to travel the world and spend more time with their loved ones. That is the essence of being financially independent. I hope to hear your story of success one day.

Lastly, thank you for reading this book!

Kelvin Wang DX

Also, check out another book by Kelvin Wang DX

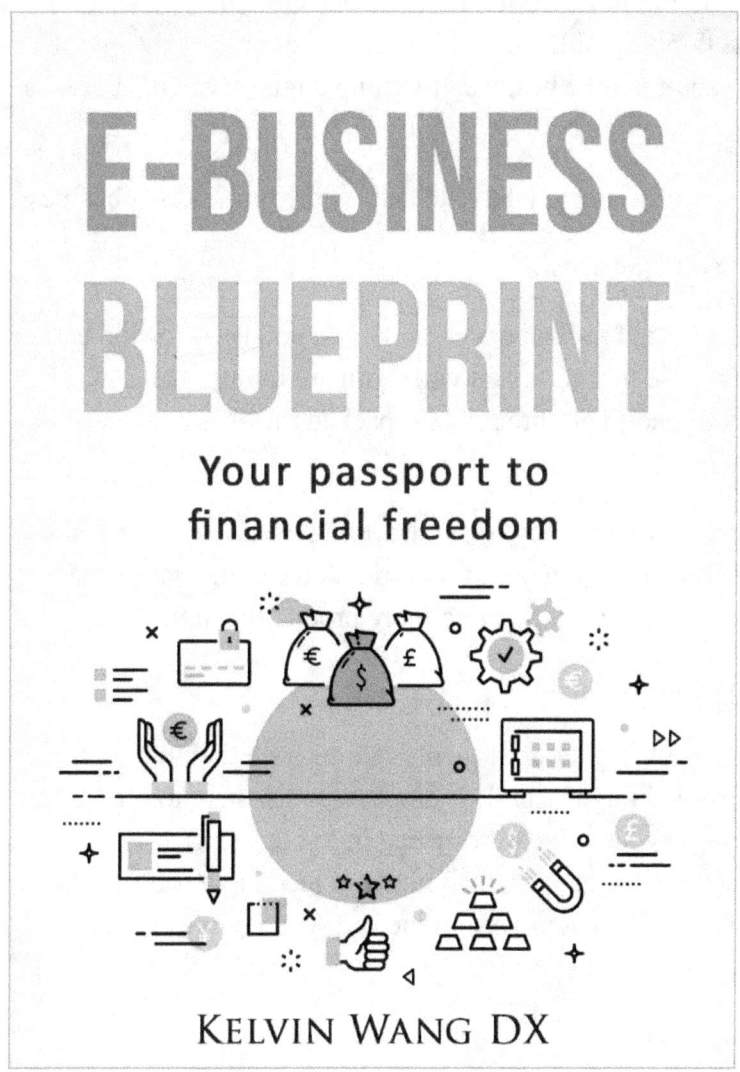

e-Business Blueprint: Your Passport to Financial Freedom

Free Bonus Preview

CHAPTER 1: Reasons for Getting Into an Online Business

People got different reasons for going into online business. But most often, online business is for people who got tired of working 8-5 or 9-6 every day. Rushing each morning for a gulp of coffee before fighting his way through traffic and hoping he could be earlier than usual!

As you realized that you are getting tired of working for someone else and you want to become your own boss, you start thinking of the possibility to make it big in the internet business. Hoping, you are right, and then the best way to set up a business with a greater chance to make it to success is to start now!

Here are just a few of the many reasons why you have to start with your internet business.

Goodbye to Traffic and Early Morning Rush

With an internet business, you don't need to rush up too early that you need to skip eating breakfast just so you can arrive in time for work. But when you are living in an overcrowded metropolis where you had to go through jam-packed traffic, stress and anxiety can be a daily part of your routine!

Online business can help you save a lot of money by not traveling every day. Count the savings you can have when you don't need to go out for work. You can likewise save your time and convert the time spent for daily trips into more productive inputs.

No Need Putting Up with a Toxic Boss

Most often people got fed up and want to get out of their work because they have a toxic person for a boss. Most often, bosses thought that their employees are there to please them all the time. This often happens when you are working in a sole proprietorship type of business or a one-man organization. Most often than not, you feed to your boss whims and schemes rather than get productive in your tasks. In the end, you feel thoroughly burnt out and find a quick way to change job.

Working at your own Pace and Time

When you are running an online business, you can be your own boss. You can work at a chosen time and place. You can even have more time to yourself and to your family. However, this can have its own drawback. So before you get out of your work, be sure your finances or the lack of will not cripple you. Proper timing is needed so your family will not suffer from your decision.

When you are free to decide for yourself whether you are going to work or not, be sure you manage your time effectively and efficiently. When you're alone to manage your time and no one is around to put pressure on you, you don't give yourself a reason to procrastinate. You need to learn to balance everything even without someone to answer to. Remember that every minute wasted is an opportunity lost in online business.

Unlimited Income Potential

Working on a regular career means putting up a cap on how much you can earn. But with online business, your ability to earn depends on how much time you want to put into your business. You can earn as much or as little as you want. The market for online business is too vast. You just learn to tap its unlimited resources and you go as far as you can.

You can target people around the world as the global market is getting bigger and bigger and more people are learning how to access the internet every day. You can work as much or as little as you choose. The marketplace for internet businesses is worldwide.

According to the later report of the Statistics portal, the number of internet users had risen up to 3.17 billion this year from 2.94 of the previous year. Isn't that market large enough to dip your toes into?

Minimal Expenses for an Office

Since you are working from the comfort of your home, you don't need to rent an office space. You will again be saving a lot on your administrative expenses compared if you are running a conventional type of business.

In setting up your business, all you need to have is your laptop or PC and low-cost hardware and software which you can even get for free online if you're just diligent enough to browse through your internet.

Bigger Chance to Achieve more for Less Work

An online business allows you to work fewer hours and achieve more. There are some business models that can be fully automated. You just have to set them up and (lo!), they can run on their own and earns you a passive income. This automation process now is widely used in the internet market. If you can't run your business on 100% automation, you can at least have it automated at 50% or more, so you can have more time for additional business to carry on.

What makes an online business unique than conventional ones is you can operate multiple businesses single-handedly. To simplify, you are operating a business that is almost next to impossible – Less capital, less time, and less effort for unlimited income streams potentials.

Common Problems you will Encounter at the Start of your Online Business

Starting your online business can be both rewarding and stimulating. However, you are sure to encounter a few problems that new entrepreneurs usually encounter. To steer clear of these issues, you must be aware of them and avoid them as they come along.

Tempting Opportunities and Resources

As you start hanging on the internet, you will be meeting a lot of opportunities along with remarkable resources to promising you great support in your online business. These products, usually software or a business opportunity, may be as great as their vendor advertise them. Nonetheless, if you jump from one opportunity to another, you will be losing your focus on your core business. It is, therefore, important that you start an online business with only what you absolutely need and have it run smoothly before getting into another. The same works with your software or any other tool.

Neglecting New Opportunities

Basically, this is the exact opposite of grabbing every opportunity that comes along. If you refuse to examine or look at any new opportunity sent your way because you have your focus set up trying to achieve a goal with a method that simply don't work, avoid overlooking the warning signs that tell you that you need to move on or move in another direction.

Doing Everything by Yourself

When you think it's better to keep all the profit, you keep trying to do everything so you can keep the money to yourself. Saving is always good for your business, but as your business develops, it will become impossible for you to embrace all the tasks. This is the time when you need to develop some way to ease up your workload. An example of these if subscribing for an auto responder that will take care of your mailing activities. Instead of manually sending letters, answering queries, the auto-responder allows you to maintain and develop relationships with your customer base and up-sell or cross-sell your products and services.

Having Too Many Choices

Affiliate marketing is a good start for an online business for you can earn as soon as someone buys from your inks. This is the reason why it is so popular with many people. Affiliate marketing method has many positive aspects but there are too many choices that it is confusing to know which to promote. Before you jump into marketing a new software by way of an affiliate program, check how much commission you can earn from it, how you can get paid, and know if there is some support you can get from the owner. It is also important to know if the product actually sells before promoting it.

The Internet is Bigger than What you Think

Having an online business doesn't mean that people will naturally visit your website and buy things that you offer. The internet is such an enormous marketplace that you need to know how to get prospective customers to visit your visit so you can have the chance to convert these visits into sales. Meaning, you need to learn how to generate website traffic by utilizing both free and paid traffic generators.

No Support from Family and Friend

Sometimes, we presume that our family and friends will be our loyal customer. Sad to say, in most cases, it doesn't usually happen especially during the start of your business. There are even cases when they will discourage you from doing online business. Though these people mean well, don't get easily swayed and let your goals and efforts get destructed. If you have set your goal and created a business plan to back it up, you have every opportunity to get successful.

Regardless of whom you are, your age, gender, technical skills, educational background, you can always start your own internet business. You can always harness whatever skill you have through various learning platforms and resources provided on the internet for a certain fee or for free.

Get your copy of e-Business Blueprint NOW!